Trailer-
Your Horse

Laura Harrison McBride

CONTENTS

There's a lot more to traveling with a horse than shoving him onto and yanking him off of a trailer. Indeed, if you've ever seen a horse manhandled onto a trailer, you've witnessed an approach so much more forceful than it needs to be — and so much less effective than it should be — that you may have decided that traveling with your horse simply isn't an option. If you can't ride Old Paint from your home barn to where you want to go, you're just not going.

Or, you might have decided that you never want to own a trailer, load your own horse, or go to a show or to a state park for a trail ride on your own; instead, you'll call a horse-transport company and let *them* load, transport, and unload your horse. The problem with that, of course, is that although the professionals may be quite adept at transporting your horse, they still have to do it, and you have to pay them for their services.

It's unfortunate that so many horse owners think in such clear-cut terms when it comes to trailering, because virtually *any* horse can be trailered safely by his owner if the owner simply attends to a few details, the most critical being teaching the horse how to load.

In this text you'll learn the loading method taught by the late Dr. Edwin Goodwin, long-time equine professor at the University of Maryland. It's a good method because it works, almost without fail. It works quickly on willing green horses; it works fairly quickly on older horses that have always been led; it works a bit more slowly on horses that have had negative loading and/or trailering experiences; and it can help your horse overcome fear, stubbornness, bad training, bad handling, bad nature, and bad horsemanship, at least insofar as loading is concerned.

On the Road Again

In today's highly mobile society, it's conceivable that in a single journey — especially as equestrian competitions continue to expand internationally — a horse will board a road vehicle, a railroad car, and an airplane. If the venue is particularly remote, boat travel may also be added to the mix. Still, despite our unmatched ability to transport our horses, often we don't give their journey a second thought, even though their safety and comfort during travel should always be a priority.

The mortality once associated with horse transport — the sort that occurred with unfortunate regularity when the New World was populated with European stock — is no longer an issue, the lower rates reflecting increasingly sophisticated techniques for managing travel stress. Good feed and management practices keep a horse in prime condition so that any losses of weight or muscle tone during transport are relatively inconsequential. In addition, vaccinations guard against germs a horse may encounter, and the design of trailers and protective equipment (such as leg wraps) gets better each year. Though sickness or injury can certainly add to a horse's level of stress during travel, it's not the main issue. Allaying a horse's fears of loading and unloading through proper training, and minimizing environmental stressors, should be our greatest concern, as these have the most significant impact on the horse's stress level and condition during and after transport.

Travel Stress, Equine Style

Studies using heart rate as an indicator of stress show that a horse's heart rate is significantly elevated while he is being loaded onto a trailer. Studies also reveal that the steeper the grade of the loading ramp, the greater the horse's stress. There are several possible explanations for this reaction:

- A horse instinctively fears dark, enclosed spaces — precisely the characteristics of the vast majority of trailers and vans.
- Steep ramps are often covered with hemp matting that can slip. They also tend to be narrow, often only as wide as the horse, so the handler cannot enter with the horse. Uncertain footing and an absent handler increase the horse's anxiety.
- A horse that has had a bad experience loading/unloading or during a trip associates this negative experience with all similar situations and equipment.
- A horse that has never been taught how to load properly and that is forcefully manhandled onto a trailer prior to a trip has negative expectations of travel.

Once a horse has been successfully loaded, environmental stressors associated with travel continue throughout the trip. The van may be too hot or too cold; the road may be rough or the driver inexperienced or careless; the hay might run out or the horse's neighbor may snap at him when he reaches for a wisp; the floor might be too hard or too slick; and the horse may simply wonder what's happening. In addition, he may not be accustomed to standing still for two hours or six hours or twelve hours. Each of these factors individually, and certainly any of them in combination, results in stress. The less stress a horse experiences during travel, the better.

The "Cue-On" Loading Technique

Dr. Goodwin is credited by many with inventing the cue-on loading technique, and he was certainly an early proponent in the United States. The basic technique, however, is nearly as old as horse transport and can be found in various guises in equine instruction books of antiquity. Dr. Goodwin spent more than thirty years teaching it to 4-H'ers, college equine science students, and private clients. And he taught it to me, his final graduate assistant.

What You Need

In the cue-on method, you use your voice, your body, and a cue to teach your horse to respond positively when you ask him to load onto a trailer. You'll use your knowledge of the process to condition your horse to do what you ask, when you ask. Be observant, heed your horse's body language, and be positive. Even the most willing, docile horse will think twice about strolling up a ramp into a dark little hole, never mind stepping up into one. When your horse agrees to do what you ask — which, in this case, goes against his instincts — he demonstrates infinite trust in you.

Patience is key. Plan to invest time and to control emotion when teaching cue-on loading. Decide how much of the process you wish to accomplish successfully at each training session, and always try to end on a positive note. For an older horse that has come to believe that loading is a horrible thing, limit the number of cues you ask him to accept at each session. If your horse is a bad loader, having him approach the trailer on cue in a straight line may be enough work for one session; having him approach the ramp on cue might be enough for the next. Never give up at the horse's insistence, no matter how frustrated you or he may be. You are in charge, not your horse. Only stop working on your own terms.

To reiterate, break up the method into manageable parts that your horse can accomplish successfully at each session, be patient, and soon he will load willingly.

The Horse's Motivation

The cue-on method involves reward but not a food reward and not letting the horse off the hook when he has only partially mastered the goals you've set for the particular session. It is more cause-and-effect than carrot-and-stick or even perform-and-reward: simply put, you cue your horse to move forward and he does so to avoid repetition of the cue.

Simple Tools

Many of Dr. Goodwin's students were self-proclaimed "animal nuts," some of whom had limited equine experience. Of these, some objected to the simple tools — a lead rope with chain and a dressage whip — that Dr. Goodwin used to teach horses to load. The naysayers assumed that such tools were inhumane, not realizing that what would be severe for a housecat is gentle for a horse. In the cue-on method, cues are given with nothing more stringent than a three-inch bit of string, and this is done mainly to demand the horse's attention. It's also used to establish dominance.

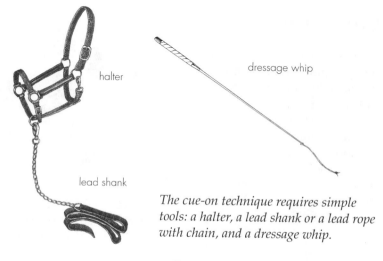

halter

dressage whip

lead shank

The cue-on technique requires simple tools: a halter, a lead shank or a lead rope with chain, and a dressage whip.

How to Cue-On Load

The cue-on loading technique is highly effective and humane. You might think that this exercise should be done in a fairly enclosed area, to keep the horse's attention, but that's not the case. It is far better to work in an open area where you cannot buy false coopera- tion from the horse and where he feels that he has an out and can flee if he really wants to. Giving him this sense of freedom will help put your horse at ease and help you gain his trust.

Equipment

Long lead rope with chain

Dressage whip

Trailer, preferably a ramp type (a step-up trailer is slightly more difficult for the horse and may require an extra session or two of work)

Getting Started

One objective of a good train- ing program is to establish a predictable routine that will put the horse at ease and help to reinforce the lessons learned. Before beginning each training session, take time to groom your horse. A thorough groom- ing will relax him and make him more receptive to the lesson that follows.

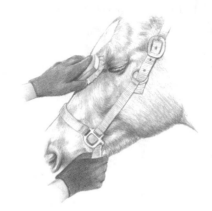

Grooming him before the training ses- sion begins establishes an enjoyable pre-lesson routine for your horse.

Walking and Halting on Cue

To train your horse to load on cue, you must first teach him to walk and halt on cue. This may be the entire lesson for the first day, depending on the age of your horse, his attention span, and his prior loading experiences. Here's how.

1. Pass the chain over the horse's nose, and hold him on the near side with the long lead rope. Pass the lead rope in front of your body and hold it in your left hand, just as you would when leading your horse; hold the dressage whip in your right hand.

2. Say "Walk," and simultaneously tap the horse on the hindquarters with the whip. If your horse doesn't move, give the command again and tap him on the hindquarters a bit more forcefully. When giving physical cues, always err on the side of too little force rather than too much. If the horse doesn't respond, repeat the command using slightly more force behind the cue. When he begins to walk, praise him warmly as you walk at his shoulder. An encouraging, enthusiastic "Good" is enough. Remember not to tug; simply walk beside him as he responds to the cue. *Note:* When giving the Walk cue, be sure to tap your horse only on the hindquarters. If he feels the whip on his legs, he may kick.

Say "Walk," and tap the horse on the hindquarters with the whip while walking beside him.

3. After walking several paces with your horse, bring him to a halt with the command "Whoa" and a fairly sharp tug on the lead. Don't pull so hard that the horse tosses his head in the air from pain or backs up to resist; instead, tug just enough to elicit the desired response. Praise him for halting.

4. Repeat this sequence several times to reinforce the cues. Common wisdom suggests that a horse learns something after two repetitions, yet each horse is different. Observe your horse for increasing confidence or for signs of boredom; both are signals that the horse is ready for the next stage.

As your horse learns the cues, you will be able to tap less insistently and tug less forcefully. Eventually, a single tap or even the verbal cue alone may be enough. Conversely, if your horse is reluctant, you will need to increase the authority of the aids until you get the response you've requested. Once a positive response is received, back off by using a gentler request.

As your horse learns what each cue means and begins to respond consistently, gradually cut back and eventually eliminate the verbal praise. By doing so, the association between the cue and response becomes automatic: when you ask for the walk, your horse gives the walk; when you ask for the halt, he halts. If you were to continue rewarding your horse with the same level of praise after he responds to each cue, the praise would come to hold little meaning for him, and you would have difficulty providing positive

---

Leading onto a Trailer?

Your horse is making progress. He now willingly walks and halts on the lead in response to a minor cue. So, you might wonder, why not just lead him onto the trailer? Won't that work every time?

Yes and no. If you choose to lead your horse onto a trailer, it will involve some degree of pulling on your part, and your horse might choose to resist, backing up and setting up the first failure to load, which would likely be followed by others. In addition, if you're in front of the horse, particularly if you are busy tugging and trying to hold him near the cross-ties or tie ring until someone snaps up the butt bar, you may have a difficult time getting out of the trailer.

reinforcement during the next phase of the maneuver, whatever it might be. When you are certain your horse knows the cues Walk and Whoa, it is time to approach the trailer.

Loading onto a Ramp Trailer

Park your trailer on level ground, preferably grass or dirt, and choose to work at a time of day when the interior of the trailer is at its brightest. As mentioned earlier, horses are naturally wary of dark, enclosed spaces, so the brighter the trailer's interior the better. Before you begin, be sure the trailer is solidly parked and doesn't sway or tip. A trailer that isn't stable will undermine your horse's confidence.

It's useful to have a helper nearby for this lesson, particularly if your horse refuses to walk straight up the ramp (see page 10), but if you are a good horseman, have boundless patience, and know your horse well, a helper isn't absolutely necessary. You'll want to pay close attention to your horse's body language during this exercise, so you'll know if and when he might choose to resist or strike out.

When training your horse to load, always end on a positive note within the horse's comfort zone, and reward him with lavish verbal praise. Training your horse to load will take at least two sessions of work and probably more.

1. Groom your horse to relax him and make him receptive to today's lesson.

2. Reinforce walking and halting on cue by revisiting steps 1–3 on pages 7–8.

3. After your horse responds successfully to the Walk and Halt cues, give the Walk command and approach the ramp calmly and purposefully. Don't lead him to the ramp; instead, walk *with* him, holding the lead rope as you cue him to walk forward by voice and a tap of the whip, if needed. Depending on the configuration of the trailer, you may have to lengthen the lead to let him walk forward alone into his space on the trailer. But that, too, is the beauty of this technique. Because he's responding to your cue to walk forward and isn't being led, this will be an easy transition.

4. When the horse reaches the ramp, he will probably balk, walk forward at an angle, stop, or back up. *If he balks*, gently nudge him back into position facing the ramp, and then tap his hindquarters with the dressage whip to cue him to walk forward. *If he walks forward at an angle*, attempting to step off the side of the ramp, position a helper with a second dressage whip on the far side of the ramp. Back the horse, and ask him to approach again. Work together with your helper, alternately tapping the horse's hindquarters if necessary. This should keep him moving straight ahead. *If he stops*, tap his hindquarters with the dressage whip and cue him again to walk forward. *If he backs up*, back him until he stops. Then stand for a brief while, let him relax, and cue him again to walk forward. If he insists on backing — some horses have learned this technique to evade loading — swat his hindquarters with the whip, using sufficient force to compel him to walk forward. *Note:* Horses don't like to back up very far and typically use the maneuver as a last-ditch evasion; choosing between backing into the sting of a whip and going forward is really no choice at all, and your horse will quickly comply.

5. It may take five, six, or even more attempts for your horse to walk onto the ramp and into the trailer. (Some horses may even need to revisit an earlier step in the process before proceeding. This is to be expected.) Once he is in, praise him warmly and touch him lightly on the hindquarters, which cues him to move forward and away from the unsecured butt bar. If he cannot go forward any farther, he will take the cue to mean, "Don't move back." You will have walked into the trailer with the horse as far as you are able, depending on the trailer configuration and the number of occupants.

Once he is loaded, touch your horse lightly on the hindquarters.

6. Once inside the trailer, the horse should appear fairly relaxed and be willing to stand still until you cue him to back out. Secure the butt bar and then the cross-ties. Remove the lead chain from the horse's halter.

Reminder

A horse that loads badly will eventually be put through far more trauma than you might inflict with a well-timed, well-intentioned swat of the whip during training. Your goal is to make your horse understand that he must walk up the ramp and onto the trailer at your cue. He also must learn that evading, by backing up or moving sideways, has unpleasant consequences.

Backing Out of a Ramp Trailer

Once the horse has loaded successfully onto the trailer, and you've praised him and secured the butt bar and cross-ties, let him stand quietly for a few minutes. Then prepare to back him out of the trailer. Enlist the help of an assistant.

1. Unfasten the cross-ties, and reattach the lead chain to the horse's halter.

2. Have your helper unlatch the butt bar and then stand at the side of the ramp, where the horse will back off.

3. With your hand, touch your horse's flank gently, even with just the tips of your fingers. This is a "guiding" touch to help guide him back, keep him straight, and maintain his trust, rather than the stronger, more positive "stop" touch used earlier. Say "Back," and praise him when he has come completely off the trailer and is standing quietly, awaiting further instructions.

How Long Does It Take?

You may think that this whole process will involve only two sessions of work for you and your extremely talented horse — one for walking and halting on cue and one for loading on cue. Anything is possible, but such swift success is likely only if your horse is a trusting, willing pupil, hasn't had previous negative experiences (loading *or* training), and you have the right attitude and sufficient persistence to work patiently through each step until he performs it correctly.

Most horses require more than two sessions to learn to load properly. Because a horse's attention span is fairly short, consider breaking down the training process into manageable mini-sessions such as this:

- **Session 1:** Walk and halt on cue
- **Session 2+:** Walk up to the ramp on cue (as many times as needed to instill confidence in your horse)
- **Session 3+:** Walk up the ramp and into the trailer on cue (as many times as needed to instill confidence in your horse)

Pay special attention to your horse's body language during each session, never push him beyond his comfort level, and always end on a positive note. The horse may get halfway up the ramp, back off quickly, then turn sideways. In such a case, straighten him out and repeat the loading cue. If the horse is slightly more successful on the next attempt — say he pokes his head into the trailer before backing out, for example — repeat the loading cue and stop him at the place where he is still comfortable. Praise him with an enthusiastic "Good boy," then quit for the day. Don't give food treats, as you'll be out of luck one day if you need to load your horse and don't have any food rewards handy. Verbal praise works best, and a pat or stroke is also appropriate.

When resuming training, repeat what was done successfully during the previous session. Your horse's confidence and comfort level should improve with repetition during each session.

Loading onto a Step-Up Trailer

Because a step-up trailer is far more challenging for the horse to negotiate, both physically and mentally, than a ramp trailer, I recommend training horses to load onto a ramp trailer first, if possible. When your horse is confident and comfortable loading onto a ramp trailer, he'll be more willing and able to negotiate a foot-high step and walk into a step-up trailer. The training process for both trailer types is more or less the same, but, generally, training a horse to load onto a step-up trailer takes at least twice as long as training to load onto a ramp trailer, mainly because the horse may be thoroughly intimidated by the step. The basic training objectives are as follows:

- Cue the horse to walk forward.
- Cue the horse to walk forward to the trailer.
- Cue the horse to walk forward and into the trailer.
- Praise horse warmly and touch him lightly on the flank.
- Secure butt bar, then cross-ties.
- Remove the lead chain from the horse's halter.

If you must begin training with a step-up trailer, be *absolutely* certain that your horse will walk forward on cue, no matter what. Then introduce him to the trailer.

Enlist the aid of two assistants to help you guide the horse on and off the trailer, but be certain both are horsepeople and thoroughly familiar with how quickly a horse can back away and wheel around. Instruct the helpers to remain alert, safe, and move out of harm's way if necessary.

1. Because on a step-up trailer there is no ramp to define how far right or left the horse can move, position one helper on either side of the trailer to define the path you want the horse to take. In effect, the helpers create a human wall or chute for the horse's progress.

2. Cue the horse to walk forward. Encourage your helpers to reach out and gently direct him onto the trailer.

3. When the horse reaches the trailer, he may automatically step up in obedience to your cue to walk forward. More likely, though, he will stop. *Never* lift a horse's front leg and place it on the trailer in an attempt to have him continue forward; this is a dangerous practice and will only confuse the horse. Instead, back him, walk away from the trailer, reinforce the Walk cue, and approach the trailer again.

4. If you get tired after a few refusals and backings, instruct one of the assistants to restart the process for you.

5. When the horse is successfully loaded, secure the butt bar, then the cross-ties. Remove the lead chain from the horse's halter.

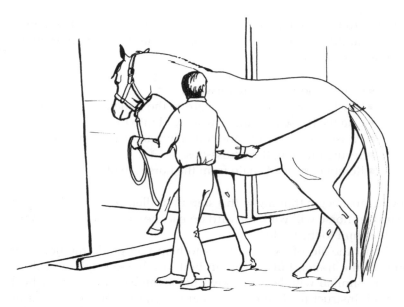

Once your horse is comfortable and confident, he will step up and walk right into the trailer at your urging, without help from assistants.

Backing Out of a Step-Up Trailer

If your horse loaded successfully onto a step-up trailer, next he must learn to back and step down. Because horses don't like to back, let alone back and step down blindly, this lesson can be quite stressful for the horse.

You'll begin as you would for backing from a ramp trailer, this time enlisting the aid of two helpers. As you did for loading, position your helpers on either side of the trailer to form a human chute. Take your position next to the horse as soon as possible, turning yourself so you face the trailer's exit.

1. Unfasten the cross-ties, and attach the lead chain to the horse's halter.

2. Have a helper unlatch the butt bar and then stand at the side of the trailer, where the horse will back off. Have the other helper stand on the opposite side.

3. Position yourself at the horse's shoulder, give the Back command, and instruct the helpers to guide the horse back with encouraging words and a gentle touch on the hindquarters. Do not use reward words (e.g., "Good boy," "Good horse," etc.) until the horse is safely off the trailer.

4. When the horse has backed and stepped down successfully, give lots of verbal praise and physical rewards, such as pats and neck rubs.

Good Footing

Because it is difficult for a horse to exit from a step-up trailer, good footing is extremely important. Always park a step-up trailer on grass or dirt, not pavement. Horses respond best to soft, familiar surfaces when unloading, especially early on. If a horse puts his hind feet down on a slick, hard surface, he might scramble, hurting himself, a handler, or a bystander. When your horse is comfortable loading and unloading, it may be safe to unload on hard surfaces, but if you have a choice park on grass or dirt. (Note: A ramp trailer should also be parked on grass or dirt, especially at first, but this is not quite so critical as it is with a step-up trailer.)

Points to Remember

Cue-on loading is a straightforward training method, but lest you be overly optimistic, keep these points in mind.

■ **You must be patient.** Everyone who trains a horse in the cue-on loading technique knows that it's not a source of instant gratification. Learned successfully, however, it leads to a lifetime of good loading for your horse.

■ **It's not a quick fix.** Don't expect a so-called bad loader to learn cue-on loading in a day because you want to go to a show; and don't expect a good lead-on loader or a green-but-not-ruined horse to learn it in a day, either. Train your horse for loading as intensively as you would train him for any other essential skill *before* you travel together.

■ **Always give the verbal command and physical cue simultaneously.** This allows your horse to associate the command with the desired response. If you were to give the physical cue before the verbal command, the horse might wonder why he's being hit and become agitated.

■ **Reward only the desired behavior.** During the training process, be careful not to talk nicely to or pet your horse when he becomes upset and does not do what you want. Such gestures of consolation only confuse the horse, causing him to think that he is being rewarded for not cooperating. Instead, use a firm, low tone, and don't yell. Think of this as your "command" voice. Repeat your cues insistently and calmly until your horse complies, no matter how upset he may seem to be. When he's performed the desired behavior, then you can reward him with verbal and physical praise.

■ **When loading, always fasten butt bar *before* the cross-ties.** If the horse is cross-tied before the butt bar is up, he could back up quickly, break the cross-ties, and injure himself or a handler.

■ **When unloading your horse, always unfasten the cross-ties *before* the butt bar.** If your horse is tied and the butt bar is down and something startles or frightens him, he may pull back, ripping the tie ring out of the trailer wall and injuring himself or you.

■ **Practice.** When you are fairly confident that your horse knows how to load and unload, practice with him several more times. Repetition reinforces learning. After reinforcing the skill, you can give it a rest until you're ready to load, particularly if you're traveling fairly soon, say within a week or two. If there are long time lags between trips, revisit the skill every few months, until the horse has been successfully loaded and hauled several times, at which point you'll be absolutely sure that he knows what to do.

■ **Keep your dressage whip handy.** Always keep your dressage whip with you when traveling, particularly for the first few road trips with your horse, just in case an old fear or doubt should get the better of him. If, for reasons beyond your control, your horse has a bad loading experience or a bad trip after learning the cue-on loading method, you may need to do a short refresher course.

Hauling Options

Whatever type of rig you choose and however many horses it can carry, the rig should be tall enough and wide enough to allow each horse to move his head about freely to maintain balance. If partitioned, each stall in the rig should be wide enough and long enough for the horse to move a step forward or backward and to shift his weight from side to side somewhat. If you can squeeze past your horse once he's loaded in the rig, the stall is probably a good size.

Horse Vans

A British horse van, or permanent horse transport, might more aptly be described as a "horse box" — in short, a stall in which horses can move about with considerable freedom, as if at home. Studies have shown that most horses experience minimal stress when traveling this way. They are free to position themselves forward, backward, or sideways, as they wish and as the van's motion dictates, thereby minimizing discomfort and cramping. Horses can fall in a horse van if the ride is bad, but careful, predictable driving and good road conditions minimize its likelihood.

Though horse vans generally offer a smooth, stable ride, their side ramps are typically steep. Horse vans are most commonly used in professional hauling, often for racehorses. At the racetrack, the ramp is extended, not from the truck's deck to the ground (which can be as much as three feet away) but to an earthen off-loading ramp that provides a gentle descent to the ground. Without that useful intermediary structure for loading and unloading, the ramp must be covered with a nonslip material, such as a hemp mat, to provide adequate traction so the horses can negotiate the ramp safely. Be sure the mat is fastened securely at top and bottom to provide solid footing. In the event of mechanical problems, horses must be off-loaded and then reloaded onto a replacement vehicle, which can be a major inconvenience.

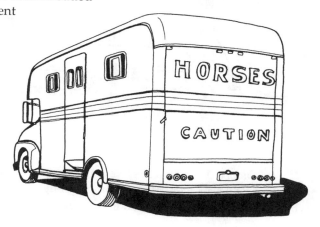

Horse Trailers

Trailers range in style from light all-aluminum carriers to heavy steel and plywood models, with a wide assortment of models in between. Your finances, tow vehicle, and horse should all be carefully considered before making a purchase. Determine how much you can reasonably spend, and then research what's most appropriate. The trailer's hitching device and configuration are also important considerations.

Among detachable trailers that require a separate towing vehicle, the basic choice is between a gooseneck and a bumper hitch, also called a *tagalong*. Each hitch type is available for various trailer styles, which you should consider carefully when choosing a trailer to suit your traveling needs. One advantage of a detachable rig is that if the towing vehicle has problems, the trailer can easily be reattached to a replacement vehicle, with no unloading of horses required.

Hitch Types

Gooseneck hitches are permanently mounted on the bed of a pickup with a large bracket. Goosenecks offer an excellent turning radius and are more stable on the road than bumper hitches. They are more expensive, however, and, pound for pound, require a heavier, more expensive towing vehicle than do bumper hitches.

gooseneck hitch

The *bumper hitch* attaches to a bumper or frame-mounted receiver on the towing vehicle. If the engine is strong enough and the tow vehicle's frame is sturdy and made of steel, pickup trucks, larger sports

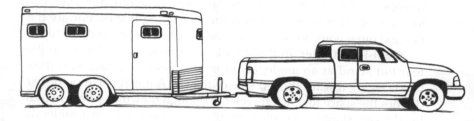

bumper hitch

utility vehicles (SUVs), and even "land yacht" types of cars, such as old full-size Cadillacs, can haul trailers with bumper hitches. (If hauling by car, a one- or two-horse trailer is the largest size you'd want to risk. Confirm your vehicle's towing capacity with a mechanic.)

Trailer Style

Once you've selected a hitch type, you must consider what trailer style will be most appropriate for you and your horse. Any trailer type can be outfitted with a ramp or a step up.

Straight-load trailer. A traditional trailer, the straight-load is available in several sizes and can accommodate from one to four horses, possibly even five. Horses generally enter side-by-side and face forward. A four-horse straight-load may place two pair of horses, one in front of the other, or in an extremely large trailer may place two horses facing the rear and two horses facing forward, with a single aisle between each pair from which the horses load and unload. If need be — and only if the flooring is sufficient and your tow vehicle is able to pull the extra weight — a pony can be hauled facing sideways in the aisle space.

Two-horse front-load trailer. In the two-horse front-load, a variation of the straight-load, horses load from the front and stand facing *away* from the direction of travel. The horses load through small ramps, on either side of the center line, that are angled to accommodate the tow bar and the tow vehicle. These trailers aren't common, but studies have shown that horses experience less stress when hauled facing away from the direction of travel, so it might be worthwhile searching for one, particularly if your horse doesn't travel well. *Warning: Never* back horses into a straight-load trailer. The load distribution is not designed for rear-facing horses, nor are the ties and other equipment. Serious and needless injury could result.

Slant-load trailer. In the slant-load, horses are loaded from the rear but stand at an angle, about 60 degrees off center, with their heads facing toward the left side of the rig. A metal partition or bar defines the space for each traveler. Although they may offer enough head room, slant-load trailers are often too narrow for warmbloods and large Thoroughbreds, unless the partitions are adjustable and can be rearranged to accommodate two larger horses in a space that might normally carry three Arabians or Quarter Horses, for example. Some slant-load trailers offer rear-facing travel (that is, 60 degrees off center, with the head facing toward the rear rather than toward the tow vehicle), but they are rare and difficult to find. Slant-loads usually have a high step up, as much as a foot from grade, in order to maintain the structural integrity required to carry so much weight in a relatively short trailer.

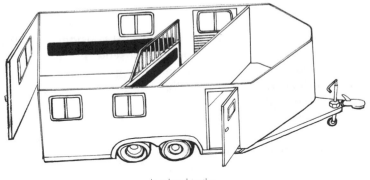

slant-load trailer

Stock trailer. In the United States, some people use stock trailers, originally intended to haul cattle, to approximate the "loose-box"–style trailering of the British horse van. Though this is fine for shorter horses, such as Arabians and old-style Quarter Horses and ponies, a Thoroughbred, Saddlebred, racing-style Quarter Horse, or warmblood will not have sufficient headroom and, therefore, won't be able to maintain proper balance. If the tall horse cannot balance properly, he may fall down, resulting in serious injury. Also, if the horse is scared and flips his head up, even while wearing a head bumper (that is, a poll protector or guard), he may die.

Stock trailers offer good ventilation, the open-slat areas providing excellent air circulation. Some horsemen who use stock trailers partially cover the openings with Plexiglas to reduce drafts and to prevent rain from entering. Others fit the trailers with partitions. Some load as many as three horses side-by-side in a front row, then install a partition and load another row of three behind. Typically, horses in a stock trailer lean on each other without much protection, so it is especially important to wrap legs and use head bumpers.

Trailers for two or four horses that have no permanent partitions are sometimes used in a similar manner when hauling a single horse. This approach can work quite well. The horse can then decide where he feels best balanced, and he probably won't upset the balance of the trailer when he adjusts his position. He also can stretch his legs and neck. The drawback is that a sudden stop could cause more serious injury to a loose horse than to one tied and held in place by leads, partitions, and a butt bar. Most typically, two horses are hauled in a two-horse trailer, three or four horses are hauled in a four-horse trailer, and so on, eliminating loose-box travel entirely.

Manger-style trailer. In a manger-style trailer, the area in front of the horse's head is boxed as storage space. That may be nice if the trailer lacks a dressing room for storage, but it will restrict the horse's ability to stretch his head down and drain his sinuses, contributing to travel stress. If you have long trips planned, a walk-through or Thoroughbred-style trailer will be a better option for your horse, even though you'll have to store items in your vehicle. (If you're hauling with a car or an SUV and you need to carry lots of hay with you, you can mount a hayrack on the roof of the trailer. And by all means, cover the hay with a tarp if bad weather is predicted.)

Safety First

Before you buy, have a mechanic inspect the trailer, especially if it's used, to confirm that all mechanical and electrical parts are in good working order. Also, check the tire condition; tires are easily replaced if worn, so don't reject a trailer solely because of its tires. Then check, or enlist the help of a knowledgeable horseman to check, the trailer's structural integrity. The floor should be solid, not warped, damp, rusty, or soft. The ramp hinges should be in good working order, not corroded or sprung. The walls should be sturdy enough to withstand hoof impact. If you prefer a thin-walled trailer but have a big horse that kicks, hang stall mats on the walls for added insurance.

Before you haul or have your horse hauled by others, always check the tires for adequate inflation and good tread. Then do a through visual inspection of the trailer's interior. Make sure there are no nails, loose wood, bent metal parts, or other protrusions that might pierce your horse. Make sure everything is loaded securely, not loose or precariously positioned, as falling and rolling objects might frighten or injure your horse. Check the hay nets; they must be securely fastened in a place accessible to the horse. Check any side half-doors or drop-down windows to be sure they will stay closed during travel. Finally, be certain that when loaded, the horse and all his parts, including his head, will remain inside the trailer at all times during travel.

Travel Equipment and Supplies

No matter what type of trailer you choose or must use when traveling, preparing your horse for the trip and packing needed supplies can help make the trip as comfortable and as stress-free as possible for your horse.

Protective Gear

Whenever your horse travels, he should be protected from bumps and cuts due to jostling and unexpected jolts in the trailer.

■ **Halter.** When trailering, *always* use a leather or breakaway halter that has a nylon body and leather crownpiece. If your horse gets himself twisted, he will be able to struggle and break free of the halter.

■ **Lead rope with chain.** Use a lead rope with a chain to load the horse. When your horse has learned cue-on loading, you no longer need the lead, but because your horse became accustomed to it during the training process, continue with what he knows. Tie with cross-ties, then remove the chain. If the trailer isn't equipped with cross-ties, switch to a lead without a chain for tying.

■ **Head bumper.** A head bumper is a good idea, particularly for tall horses being transported in short trailers. Avoid hauling in a trailer not designed for your type of horse, and always take needed precautions. Horses generally don't rear in trailers, but they might fling their heads in the air or jump a little if they are frightened. Head bumpers are designed to protect the head and are made of either dense felt or foam covered with leather or leatherlike man-made material. The head bumper attaches to the halter.

head bumper

■ **Quilts and bandages.** If you have sufficient time and are able to apply them properly — that is, not so tight that they bow tendons nor so loose that they come off and entangle your horse's feet — you can use quilts and standing bandages to protect your horse's lower legs during travel. Applying quilts (or fleece or the newer no-bow, fleece-covered, foam-filled leg wraps) and bandages can be time-consuming, so if you choose this option apply them early on the day of the trip. (If you're new to bandaging, it may take 30 minutes or more for you to complete the job. Have an experienced person check that the bandages aren't too tight when you're done.) If the horse stands quietly, an experienced bandager can do the job in as little as five to ten minutes.

1. Wrap the quilt around the leg, keeping it low and fairly snug. Secure.

2. Beginning in the middle, wrap the bandage in the same direction as you did the quilt. Leave some of the quilt visible.

3. Wrap back upward, applying a fair amount of pressure. Finish at the top, and secure with tape.

4. Wrapping the quilt and bandage low on the leg provides added protection.

■ **Shipping boots.** For spur-of-the-moment trips or if your horse is being transported by someone who is not a proficient bandager, shipping boots are a good alternative. Typically, shipping boots, which reach from just below the horse's knee to the top of the hoof, incorporate a bell-boot section that protects the coronet band. (If you use wraps and standing bandages, begin with a bell boot, applying it before you begin to wrap, so the horse won't damage the hoof wall or coronet band if he scrambles.) If you plan to use shipping boots, put them on your horse and lead him around the property a few times to get him used to how they feel *before* you ship.

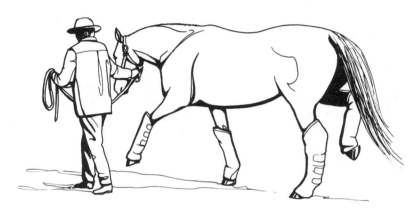

Shipping boots feel strange to a horse. Get your horse accustomed to them before you travel.

Other Provisions

It goes without saying that when traveling you must load all of your horse's standard equipment and anything extra you think you might need at his destination or for the event in which you are participating. Here are a few essentials that I never travel without:

■ **Water.** Horses are often quite particular about their water, so stow some five-gallon jugs of their regular water, just in case. Adding Kool-Aid to strange water is said to make it palatable for horses, so you may want to bring some of that along as well. At home, an adult horse can drink 10 to 20 gallons of water per day. Generally, horses drink less during travel, but a minimum of 10 gallons per day per horse should be enough.

- **Hay and feed.** Never change your horse's hay or feed immediately before or after a trip. If you are traveling to a new barn, bring along some of his regular hay and grain — enough for several days. Use his standard ration for the first day or two, then mix it gradually with what his new home offers. Changing food gradually in this way minimizes your horse's gastric distress. Before, during, and after travel, be sure your horse has good-quality hay to keep his gut active, something partially helped by daily exercise when he's not traveling.
- **Hay nets.** For trips that take longer than an hour, and particularly if you're headed to a horse show where the horse may stand in or be tied to the trailer for most of the day, be sure you load hay nets to capacity, so he can nibble to pass the time and keep his gut active.
- **Fly sheets, coolers, and sweat sheets.** These can be useful extras, particularly if you're traveling out of your immediate area.
- **Treats.** Always have a generous supply of your horse's favorite treats available.

Creature Comforts

When your horse can load successfully and you've packed all needed equipment, you've got about 90 percent of the trailering battle won, at least as far as your horse is concerned. But there are a few other considerations that deserve your attention, which may greatly improve your horse's comfort during travel.

- **Ensure adequate ventilation.** Adequate ventilation protects against excessive stress during transport. Stuffy enclosed areas, such as a poorly ventilated trailer, not only contribute to your horse's physical stress, they also encourage the spread of airborne pathogens and can increase the risk for developing respiratory illness. If you must use different trailers, familiarize yourself with them before you travel, and consult their owners for advice regarding the best window/vent arrangements.

When making adjustments to a trailer's ventilation, angle the vents in such a way that the incoming air doesn't blow directly on your horse. One of the best ways to determine airflow is to adjust the vents, hop in the trailer (with no horses loaded), and have someone tow it around the farm property so you can feel for yourself how much air is entering and where the air travels. In addition, observe your horse after a few local trips. Has his mane blown to the opposite side? Is he trying to huddle against one side or other of the trailer?

■ **Allow sufficient slack in the lead.** Unless you must tie the horse's head close to the trailer wall — because he is next to a fighting horse, for example — don't run the lead short. When tied, your horse should be able to drop his head enough to allow for proper drainage of the sinuses, which helps to prevent buildup of harmful microorganisms and dust. If your horse can drop his head to the point of a grazing posture when tied, the lead is too long and must be shortened. A long lead is dangerous for the horse at all times when traveling, but especially during a sudden, unexpected stop.

■ **Provide sufficient bedding.** My very tall horse (16.3 hands high) lifts his tail and lets fly about five minutes down the road. I've always assumed that the trailer's motion relaxes him because he is a good traveler, but such ready defecation might just as easily be an expression of nerves. Whichever the case, be sure to provide sufficient bedding for your horse and monitor your horse's bodily functions closely during travel. Some horses simply refuse to urinate in a trailer; others urinate a lot. Both can be problematic for different reasons. Be vigilant during your first few road trips, carefully assessing your horse's condition before and after travel. If you suspect your horse is losing condition, even on short trips, consult your veterinarian for possible solutions.

■ **Try a special browband.** On a hot day, you might want to install a wettable visor on your horse's browband to keep him cool. Or, you might try a magnetic browband, which some equine massage therapists and acupuncturists swear by as effective tools for relaxing horses. It is believed that the magnetic field produced by the browband alters the way certain molecules important to cell function act within the brain, thereby stimulating the production of calming hormones such as melatonin. For best results, a magnetic browband should be applied at least an hour before travel.

Seasonal Strategies

On a trip of any length, plan to check the horses at least every three hours to be sure that they have hay and have not gotten untied or entangled in a fallen hay net. If you know that a trip will take longer than six hours, plan ahead and research a safe place to unload the horses to let them graze and stretch their necks for 15 to 20 minutes.

Summer travel. In summer months, adequate ventilation is relatively easy to achieve. Just leave the windows and any top closure above a rear-facing ramp open. And keep the rig moving. Carry five-gallon containers of your horse's usual water, and offer it each time you stop, preferably in a familiar bucket. How many jugs you'll need depends on your horse's drinking habits, so observe them carefully before a trip, and load water accordingly.

If you stop to eat and refuel, try to park in the shade, open the tops of hay doors if you have them, and make your stop as short as possible.

Winter travel. In winter, many people are inclined to keep a trailer or van tightly closed in an effort to make it warm and cozy for their horse. This is a mistake, because if your trailer is closed tightly you simply cannot provide your horse with adequate ventilation and he will be too warm. Dr. Goodwin was fond of telling his students that horses lived outside successfully, in all sorts of weather, for fifty-five million years without any help from humans, and he'd just as soon have seen all horses living outside virtually all of the time, unless they were sick or injured. And even then outdoor living had its benefits. So don't coddle your horse.

If you see condensation forming on the windows, you can be sure that the trailer or van is too hot and damp, and the horses are uncomfortable. By not providing adequate ventilation, you inadvertently create an environment that does more harm than good.

Tip for Winter Blanketing

In winter, be careful not to blanket your horse too heavily during transport. Blanket your horse appropriately for his clipped or unclipped state and the day's temperature. Then before loading your horse, physically stand in the trailer wearing proper attire for the weather outside. If you are slightly uncomfortable — perhaps a bit chilly — in the trailer or van, it's probably just the right temperature for your horse. If you're comfortable or warm, it's probably too warm for your horse and you should adjust the vents to allow in more air. Remember, he is always wearing a fur coat.

Documentation

There's nothing more unnerving than not having the papers you need when you need them most. When traveling with your horse, make it a point to bundle up these documents, just in case. Keeping all of your important papers in a flexible file is a good idea.

■ **Negative Coggins test.** When traveling with your horse, make sure that you or the hauling company (if your horse is being shipped professionally) has a current negative Coggins test on hand for your horse. The Coggins test determines whether the horse is a carrier of equine infectious anemia; a negative test indicates that the horse is not a carrier and poses no risk of spreading the disease.

■ **Current health certificate.** Some states require a current health certificate in addition to a negative Coggins, so check with the Department of Agriculture in your state before you cross state lines.

The Threat of Shipping Fever

The incidence of strangles, or "shipping fever" — a highly contagious infectious disease caused by *Streptococcus equi* that occurs most commonly in horses transported long distances (more than 500 miles in one trip) — has diminished greatly in the last quarter century. The decline clearly has much to do with vaccines and other preventive strategies, such as improved feed and disinfecting trailers after each trip.

Characterized by high temperature (103°–104°F), nasal discharge, cough, difficulty swallowing, and swollen lymph glands that may abscess and burst, strangles is principally spread by direct contact with nasal secretions or pus draining from an abscess. Interestingly, *S. equi* is found in just about every stool sample taken from horses, whether or not the horses show signs of disease. Stress, which negatively affects the immune system, may be all that is necessary to allow the incubating bacterium to take hold, successfully combating the horse's weakened immune system to cause obvious signs of disease. A lengthy, stressful road trip may increase your horse's susceptibility to *S. equi*. Treatment includes penicillin and excellent care, specifically clean water and feed, a dry stall, good sanitation, and peace and quiet.

- **Insurance papers.** When hauling long distances, especially, you may want to bring your insurance papers — for horse and vehicle — along for the ride.
- **Contact information and contingency plans.** In case of an emergency, particularly if you become injured or incapacitated during the trip or at a show, it's a good idea to carry with you contact information and contingency plans so people will know whom to contact and what to do.
- **Recovery information.** If your horse had been tattooed or has had a chip implanted to prevent theft and to facilitate recovery efforts, you may wish to carry that information along with you, specifically the identification number itself and any documentation your veterinarian provided.
- **Records and registration.** If you are going to a show and need proof of the horse's prior performance or size (pony papers, for example) or breeding (registration for a breed show), stow copies of that information, too.

Rules for the Road

In some states, a commercial driver's license is required if you plan to haul anything larger than a two-horse trailer. Check with your state's registry of motor vehicles before planning a cross-country trip with Sir Speedo. And always observe these simple rules of the road when hauling.

- **Don't exceed your rig's hauling capacity.** Know what it is and the weight of all horses to be loaded *before* you travel.
- **Check tire pressure for adequate inflation.** Do this the day before you travel in case you must repair or replace tires.
- **Load properly.** If you are loading one horse into a two-horse trailer, load him on the left so his weight is over the crown of the road, rather than on the lower shoulder at the edge of the road. If you're loading two horses, put the larger one on the left, again to keep the greatest weight toward the road's crown rather than toward its sloping shoulder. In the event of poorly maintained road surfaces or the need for defensive driving maneuvers, this may help to prevent a rollover.
- **Drive well.** Remember that you're hauling precious cargo that's standing in the trailer behind you. Drive carefully, being considerate

of your horse and other drivers. Make no jackrabbit starts or stops. As a general rule, leave at least one car-length in front of you for each ten miles of speed you are traveling. With a trailer adding pushing weight from behind, that's the minimum allowable distance you must maintain if you wish to make a good, safe stop, and even then a stop on demand will likely toss the horses a bit.

When turning, slow down, and be sure you have sufficient room to make a wide turn. It's a good idea to practice turning and other basic maneuvers with an empty trailer *before* hauling horses.

When you're driving on the highway, realize that a semi that passes you will produce enough drag on your truck and rig to challenge your driving skills. Be prepared to compensate for such buffeting by skillful handling. Always keep two hands on the wheel.

■ **Monitor mirrors.** Large mirrors are essential for both sides of the towing vehicle. They allow you to see beyond the towing vehicle to the trailer itself and should be monitored regularly as you drive. You'll be able to see if a horse manages to get a body part outside the trailer, which can have tragic consequences. You'll also be able to see the semi bearing down on you and will be able to react accordingly.

More Travel Tips

A few final reminders:

■ Until you understand that when you back and steer left, your rig turns right, look for drive-through spaces at shows or rest stops when you park.

■ Carry water for horses to drink and water for people to drink.

■ Carry snacks for horses and people. Horses can eat their snacks (i.e., hay) as they travel, but for safety sake you should eat snacks only when you've stopped. Eating while driving increases the risk for accidents.

■ Carry first aid kits for horses and people.

■ Carry a cell phone, fully charged, but with a vehicle power cord as well. If you must use the phone, pull into a rest area and stop the vehicle. Using a cell phone while driving in a car increases the likelihood of an accident by 30 percent. Factoring in the challenges of managing a rig carrying horses, the risk only increases. Don't do it.

Don't Double Up

For simplicity's sake, you might be tempted to bridle your horse and then slip the halter over the bridle before you travel. Don't do it. Your horse could catch the bridle inside the trailer and do serious damage to his mouth. The bridle also would interfere with hay consumption during the trip.

When You Reach Your Destination

After safely reaching your destination, back your horse out of the trailer, let him graze on the lead, if possible, or walk him for at least fifteen minutes. Once your horse is comfortable and relaxed, you're ready to tack up and mount.

Bolt-Free Bridling

Sometimes it's impossible to bridle a horse in a trailer, and many horses don't cooperate if they must be bridled in an open space. By following these simple steps, you'll be able to bridle your horse with ease at any location, and at no time will he think he is free and able to escape. You'll loop the lead over his head in two places to "secure" him while you bridle him.

1. Before you slip the halter off, prepare to apply a lead halter. Stand on the near side of the horse, at his head, close enough to reach under his jaw with your right hand.

2. Unlatch or unbuckle the leather halter. Before you let it slip down onto your left hand, or before a helper grabs it, with your right hand pass the nonchain end of the lead away from you, under the horse's throatlatch, and back up over his poll. Rest your right hand on his nose, a few inches above the nostrils, grasping and holding the lead at that point. Basically, you are creating a figure eight around his poll and nose.

3. Run the end of the lead away from you, over his nose, where the noseband of a halter would rest.

4. Bring the end of the lead back under his nose, grasping it and the loose length of halter hanging from the near side of the horse's head with your right hand. The lead forms a loose figure eight that you now grasp in the middle.

5. Slip the reins over his head with your left hand, grasping the crownpiece of the bridle at the same time. Alternatively, have a helper slip the reins over the horse's head while you hold the top of the bridle.

6. Slide the bridle up as you normally do, positioning the bit under his mouth and slipping it in, all with your left hand. Slip the crownpiece over one ear, bringing the ear forward, and then prepare to let the temporary hand-held halter slip away as you use your right hand to slide his near-side ear through the bridle.

step 6

7. Release the lead, which will drop to your horse's feet. Then latch or buckle the halter.

Mounting

If you are traveling to a show, always bring and use a mounting block. After loading and hauling your horse, and putting on his tack carefully with the least possible fuss and muss on his part, don't take any chances when mounting. Imagine your horse's confusion if you go through all that work, only to swat him up against a car bumper so you can clamber aboard. And you certainly wouldn't want to bounce down on his back after an inadequate leg up. If bystanders are pressed into groom service, you might even be foisted up and over — how embarrassing!

It's incredibly demanding to travel with your horse. But the rewards are worth the effort, particularly when your horse loads on cue, travels safely and comfortably with minimal stress, and maintains his condition.